"I have known Roy
he showed this cool ...... I started reading
through it. I knew this book needed to be published. Roy has
cooked dinners for us from recipes that are in the book and they
are very easy to follow. This is not an ordinary cook book. The
hints, tips, sick room, and other information make this book very
interesting. I hope that he will decide to do a second book in
the future."

Kathy Landis, Retired from IBM/AT&T

"Roy is an eclectic cook. I have witnessed his enthusiasm in
preparation of a meal. He has the tenacity to try different things
and the expertise to modify his most trusted recipes. His cook
book is a true evaluation of his may talents. He has gathered
antique recipes which are curious and sometimes odd, but they
work. These are time treasured relics handed down from previ-
ous generations to concoct the wizardry that became staples for
their delectable palates. The book as a whole is amusing, infor-
mative and realistic."

Grace Delos-Santos, Retired Software Analyst

"This cook book captures the true essence of Canadian culture in
a northern town. Through the simple ingredients that are both
earthly and rustic, the comfort foods sooth the mind, body and
soul. Eating a healthy dish after a long cold day revives your
senses and your inner spirit.

Peter Koutroulakis, Owner, the Old Bank
Bistro Restaurant, Fort Erie, Ontario, Canada

ART'S
OLD CANADIAN
RECIPES

ART'S
OLD CANADIAN
RECIPES

RECIPES FROM, EARLY SETTLERS,
BUSHMEN, PROSPECTORS, TRAPPERS,
HUNTING & FISHING GUIDES

ARTHUR R. THORNTON

TATE PUBLISHING & *Enterprises*

Published by Tate Publishing & Enterprises, LLC
127 E. Trade Center Terrace | Mustang, Oklahoma 73064 USA
1.888.361.9473 | www.tatepublishing.com

Tate Publishing is committed to excellence in the publishing industry. The company reflects the philosophy established by the founders, based on Psalm 68:11,
"The Lord gave the word and great was the company of those who published it."

Book design copyright © 2009 by Tate Publishing, LLC. All rights reserved.
Cover design by Kellie Southerland
Interior design by Tyler Evans

Published in the United States of America

ISBN: 978-1-60696-309-8
1. Cooking : Regional and Ethnic
09.03.30

GETTING BACK TO BASICS

By A. R. Thornton
How It All Got Started

A few years ago while rushing home from one of our many shopping trips, my wife and I started talking about how nice it would be to find some way to slow down and enjoy life a little more. Stop and think about it: back and forth to work every day, TV, running here and there. Before you know it, your life is rushing by. Not to mention the foods we eat. Next time you come home from shopping, read the labels. We realized that life was too precious, and we would start making some changes. We thought, *Let's get back to basics*, but how?

One sure way would be by putting in a garden. Once

this was done and everything started coming up, we thought we would do some canning and even try some pickles. So for the next few weeks we started looking for some good recipes to use, and don't get me wrong, there are a lot of good recipes out there you can use, but they were not the ones for us, for a lot of good reasons, so we kept looking.

Then one day it came to me. I remembered my mom and dad making just about everything they needed for our family and home many years ago. Then I got thinking about the old trunks with books, papers, pictures, and other family articles that we stored away many years ago after both my parents passed away. Back in those days they did not throw anything away, everything was valuable to them. And what we found could not have made us happier. What we did find was all of my mom and dad's old family recipes, some dating back to the 20's and 30's. Over the past few years we have tried and still use many of these old recipes today.

My parents settled down in a small rural town surrounded by many types of ethnic farming back in the 30's; it brought together many families by means of church socials, weddings, funerals, and fraternal organizations, so this allowed them to try and trade many old family recipes. We couldn't be happier that we found most of ours, satisfying our family and a lot of our friends and neighbors with our newfound treasures from the past.

My family today is still using and making most of these old recipes; even my grandson loves to pitch in and help. Most of these old recipes are easy to make and are also cheaper in most cases to make. They are so much better for you. Just read the labels on what you buy in the stores today. At least you know what your family is eating, because your family made it. Some of these old recipes we have are long forgotten or lost by most families today, and that's a shame because I think we should all try and get our families back to the basics of life. We did, and we love it.

Being caught up in this racing pace of everyday life, we have all but forgotten the smells, tastes, and warm love that came from the kitchens of a lifestyle we almost forgot about and lost. After forty-five years, it's great to be back and enjoying all of these delicious foods over again.

I dedicate this book
to my parents
Art and Jean Thornton

Because of their Love, Guidance, Treasures,
and Memories this book was possible

CONTENTS

PREFACE

Over the past thirty years I have collected close to fifty recipe books. I might add that a few of them I use from week to week, and each book will have a recipe that we always seem to go back to. Like our family, maybe you have a recipe that a friend has passed on to you over the years. I am sure that we all have that special family recipe that was handed down to us. We cling to and use those special recipes because they work. The nutritional value is better for you too, and that's why we take the time to make it.

Three years ago I made up my mind to make life a little simpler for us, as far as foods and the preparation of foods were concerned. The first step would be to go back to the basics of foods, and the basics of food preparation for storing. We did and still do to this day; it's easy and rewarding. With a little help from your family, you will be surprised at how fast it can be done. Most often we will buy a recipe book and have found a recipe or two that become a favorite. We feel that by taking the time to prepare good and nutritional foods for our family, it's not only better for you, but it is fun to make together. Take the time to read the labels on what you buy in stores today! So with that in mind I decided to make my own recipe file, rather than jumping from book to book or looking for a piece of paper with a recipe on it. (I'm sure we have all done that a few times.) So I started by putting together all our old traditional family recipes. We found these recipes in an old trunk, after both my parents had passed on. My family and I still use quite a few of the recipes from day to day and will continue to do so for years to come. The origin of many of these recipes is quite old. They, no doubt, were handed down from family to family, or by early settlers, Bushmen, prospectors, and trappers and through the years have been changed to suit the home kitchen. Even you will make changes. No doubt, after you have used many of these recipes, I would not recognize them as the original. This is the way it should be. It is creative, and that is how recipes are made.

The use of a recipe.

Before starting to cook, read the recipe carefully, and then read it again. It has been said that a good cook can read a recipe and decide by its contents whether it will be enjoyed or not.

USEFUL INFORMATION

Table of Fruit Yields

Apples, 1 pound—1½ to 3 C. diced, 1½ C. applesauce
Apricots, 1 pound—3 C., cooked
Bananas, 1 pound—2 C., sliced
Berries, 1 quart—3½ C.
Cherries, 1 pound—1 quart—2 ¾ C., stemmed and pitted
Figs, dried—1 pound 2 ¾ C., chopped
Grapefruit, one—2/3 to ¾ C. juice—1¼ C., diced
Peaches, 1 pound—2 to 2½ C., sliced
Pears, 1 pound—2½ C., cooked
Pineapple, one—2½-3 C., diced
Plums, 1 pound—2 C., cooked
Prunes, 1 pound—4 C., cooked—2 C., cooked and pitted
Rhubarb, 1 pound—2 C., cooked

Oven Guide

Slow Oven:	275 F-325 F	Custards, sponge cakes, fruit loaves, meats
Moderate Oven:	325 F-375 F	Cakes, some muffins, cake, desserts
Fairly Hot Oven:	375 F-425 F	Muffins, yeast breads, most cookies
Hot Oven:	425 F-500 F	Tea biscuits, pastries

Baking chart
(approximately), degrees in F

Slow oven	250–325
Moderate oven	350–375
Mod. hot oven	375–400
Hot oven	400–450
Very hot oven	450–500
Pastry Shell	450 for 12 to 15 min.
Two-crust pie/ uncooked filling	450 for 10 min. reduced to 350—30 to 35 min.
Two-crust pie/ cooked filling	440–450 for 30 min.
Custard pie	450 for 10 min.
Custard pie/reduce to	350 for 25 min.
Meringue topping	350 for 10 to 12 min.

Yeast breads	400–425 for 40 to 45 min.
Sweet rolls	375 for 15 to 20 min.
Muffins	425 for 20 to 25 min.
Biscuits	450 for 15 to 20 min.
Corn breads	425 for 20 to 30 min.
Gingerbreads	425 for 40 to 50 min.
Angel and sponge cakes	325, then to 375 for 5 min.
Loaf cake	350–375 for 40 to 50 min.
Layer cake/cupcakes	350–375 for 20 to 30 min.
Cookies, depending on size	350–425 for 6 to 12 min.

approx.	approximately
sm.	small
pt.	pint
med.	medium
gal.	gallon
sq.	square
min.	minutes
pkg.	package
C.	cup
T.	tablespoon
t.	teaspoon
lb.	pound
qt.	quart (4 C.)
lg.	large (29 oz.)
oz.	ounce

BREADS, ROLLS, AND PASTRY

Before you start your recipes for breads, rolls, or any yeast recipe, always remember that flour should be at a warm temperature. Scald milk, then let cool to luke-warm before using.

If you would like bread a little more finely textured, let dough rise in a little cooler place.

Use milk, and it will give you a softer crust and a richer golden brown.

White Bread

2 C. water
1/3 C. white sugar
1 C. milk
1/3 C. shortening
1 C. potato water
2 t. salt

Mix and heat all ingredients together to boiling point. Cool to lukewarm, then add two pkg. yeast and 10 to 11 C. flour, add 1/3 of flour and beat until smooth, then add the rest. Put on floured board and knead for four to five minutes, return to bowl. Cover with clean cloth and let rise till doubled. Have the dough a little sticky. Return to board and punch down, and knead again. Cut to size and place in greased bread tins. Let rise till double, then bake at 350 to 375° about one hour.

Art's Homemade Bread

½ T. sugar
2 pkg. yeast
¼ C. warm milk. Mix and let rise, then add the following:
2 t. sugar
¼ C. lard, melted
2 T. salt
12 to 15 C. flour
3 ¾ C. warm milk

On floured board, knead for five minutes, let rise till doubled. Punch down and let rise again. Make loaves and bake at 350° until light brown.

Donuts

¾ C. milk
¼ C. warm water
¼ C. sugar
1 pkg. yeast
1 t. salt
1 egg, beaten
¼ C. butter
3½ C. flour

Scald milk and stir in butter, salt, and sugar. Let stand until lukewarm. Add water to large bowl, sprinkle in the yeast, and let dissolve. Then add milk mixture, egg, and half the flour. Beat until smooth. Stir in flour until you have a smooth, elastic dough. Turn on to floured board and knead for 10 minutes. Cover in a bowl and let rise, until doubled. Punch down and roll out to ½ inch, cut with donut cutter. Place donuts on floured cookie sheet, let rise again. Deep fry in oil at 375°. Dip in white sugar or glaze with 2 C. powdered sugar and 1/3 C. milk, and 1 t. vanilla.

Waffles

3 C. sifted flour
1 t. baking powder
1 t. soda
1 t. salt
3 eggs, separated
2 C. sour cream
1½ C. water
3 T. melted lard

Mix all dry ingredients first, then add egg yolks, sour cream, and melted lard. Mix until smooth, add water. Beat egg whites stiff and fold into batter. Bake in hot waffle iron.

Cinnamon Rolls

1½ C. milk, heat to lukewarm
1 C. mashed potatoes
2 t. salt
2/3 C. shortening
2 eggs
½ C. water
2 pkg. yeast
1 C. sugar
6 to 8 C. flour

Add yeast to warm water for a few minutes, then add all the rest of the ingredients. Mix and let rise until doubled, punch down and roll out. Roll out like jelly roll and cut in pieces. Place on greased pan and let rise till doubled. Bake at 400° for about 25 to 30 minutes.

Refrigerator Rolls

2 eggs, beaten
½ C. milk, lukewarm
1 pkg. yeast
2 C. warm water
¾ C. sugar
1 C. lard
8 to 9 C. flour

Mix well and store in cool place. When ready to use, shape into rolls, let rise until double. Bake at 350° for about 15 to 20 minutes.

Mom's Biscuits

2 C. flour
½ t. salt
2 T. baking powder
½ t. cream of tarter
1 T. sugar
½ C. shortening
2/3 C. milk
½ t. salt

Sift dry ingredients. Cut into shortening until you have coarse crumbs. Add milk and stir until dough balls up.

Roll out about ½ inch. Cut with cutter and place on cookie sheet. Bake at 450° for 10 to 12 minutes.

Remember: Your pastry will be flakier if you put 1 T. of lemon or orange juice in as part of your liquid.

Dinner Rolls

1 pkg. yeast
1 T. sugar
3 eggs
1 C. warm water

Beat eggs in water, add sugar and yeast, mix, then let stand for 10 minutes.

Add
½ C. sugar
½ C. shortening
½ t. salt
5 C. flour

Mix and knead well. Put in the refrigerator overnight. Next day cut into two parts and roll out in 12-inch circle, cut into wedges, and roll up starting at wide end, let rise a few hours. Bake at 400° for about 15 minutes. Brush with butter and serve.

Potato Rolls

2 C. milk, scalded

½ C. sugar

2 eggs

1 T. salt

1 C. mashed potatoes

½ C. shortening

8 to 10 C. flour

2 pkg. yeast, dissolved in ½ C. warm water

Pour scalded milk over shortening, salt, sugar, and mashed potatoes, mix well and let cool to lukewarm. Dissolve yeast in warm water and add to first mixture and blend in. Then add eggs and flour, knead until smooth. Let rise until doubled in size. Shape into rolls and let rise again. Bake at 350° for about 20 to 25 minutes.

Lunch Rolls

1 C. oatmeal
2 C. boiling water
3 T. butter
¾ C. brown sugar
2 T. white sugar
2 pkg. yeast
1 T. salt
1/3 C. warm water
4 to 5 C. flour

Mix oatmeal and butter in boiling water and let cool to lukewarm. Soak yeast in lukewarm water for five minutes, then add to oatmeal mixture. Mix in rest of ingredients, cover, and let rise until doubled, then knead down and roll out on floured board, roll out to ¼ inches by 12 by 18 inches. Brush with butter and sprinkle with extra brown sugar, roll up and cut ½ inch. Place on pan and let rise until double in size. Bake at 350° for about 20 to 30 minutes.

Whole-Wheat Bread

Add 1 pkg. yeast to ½ C. warm water. Scald 1 C. milk, let cool to lukewarm.

½ C. brown sugar

1 C. cool water

1 T. salt

4 C. white flour

¼ C. lard, melted

2 C. whole-wheat flour

Pour hot milk over sugar, salt, and lard. Mix until melted, then add yeast and water. Work in flour until dough is not sticky. Make loaves and bake at 350° for 50 to 60 minutes.

Bubble Bread

1 C. milk, scalded

½ C. sugar

1 t. salt

Mix well and let cool to lukewarm. Add 2 pkg. yeast and 2 beaten eggs and blend well. Add about 4½ C. flour. Knead until smooth, not sticky. Place in greased bowl and cover with damp cloth, let rise till doubled. Punch down and let rise again till doubled. Punch down and let rise for 10 minutes. Melt 1 stick of butter in small pan. Mix 1 C. sugar and 1 T. cinnamon in a dish. Make walnut-sized dough balls, roll in melted butter then in sugar mixture. Place in angel-food cake pan in staggered rows until all dough is used. Let rise, then bake at 350° for about 45 minutes.

Cornbread

3 eggs
1 T. baking powder
1 ¾ C. flour
¾ C. shortening
1½ C. corn meal
1 ¾ C. milk
2½ T. sugar
Pinch of salt

Mix all ingredients and pour into buttered pan. Bake at 375° for 20 to 25 min. or until done.

SALAD DRESSINGS AND SAUCES

French Dressing I

1 C. sugar
¾ C. salad oil
½ C. vinegar
½ C. ketchup
½ C. salad dressing
1/8 t. celery salt
1 t. salt
1 t. Worcestershire sauce
¼ t. paprika
½ t. Tabasco sauce
1 clove garlic
1 small onion

Put all ingredients in blender for two minutes until smooth.

French Dressing II

1 C. condensed tomato soup
1 C. sugar
½ C. vinegar
½ C. vegetable oil
1 t. salt
1 t. dried mustard
1 t. celery salt
1 t. onion salt
½ t. paprika

Mix all ingredients in blender or shake in jar, store in refrigerator.

Good Mayonnaise

1 egg
1 T. sugar
1 t. salt
1 t. mustard
1/8 t. paprika
¼ C. vinegar
½ C. salad oil
1 C. water
6 t. cornstarch

In bowl, place egg, seasoning, oil, and vinegar, but do not beat. Make a thick, smooth paste by cooking cornstarch and water. Add the hot paste to ingredients in bowl, beat briskly until a thick mayonnaise results.

Mexican Dressing (for tossed salads)

1 med. onion, chopped
2/3 C. sugar
1/3 C. vinegar
½ t. celery seed
2 t. mustard
1 C. salad oil
½ t. salt

Mix all ingredients in blender for 3 minutes.

Poppy Seed Dressing

3 C. oil
2 C. sugar
1 C. vinegar
2 T. onion
2 T. mustard
2 T. poppy seed

Mix in blender until smooth and creamy.

Russian Dressing

1 C. vegetable oil
½ C. vinegar
1 C. sugar
1 t. salt
1 t. pepper
¾ C. ketchup
2 t. lemon juice
1 small onion
½ t. paprika
1 t. garlic salt
Mix in blender for 2 minutes

Taco Salad

1 head lettuce, shredded
1 onion, diced
4 tomatoes, diced
4 oz. grated cheese
7 oz. bag taco chips, crushed
1 lb. hamburger
1 can kidney beans, 15 oz. can
¼ t. salt
1 t. chili powder
Dash of Tabasco sauce
Brown hamburger, add kidney beans, salt, chili powder, and Tabasco sauce. Simmer 10 minutes and drain. Toss

together first five ingredients, then add the hot drained mixture to the tossed salad. Serve immediately with French dressing.

Blue Cheese Dressing

4 oz. blue cheese
1 C. mayonnaise
10 oz. sour cream
1 t. finely chopped onion
½ t. Worcestershire sauce
2 cloves minced garlic
¼ C. minced parsley

Mash blue cheese in a bowl and blend all remaining ingredients into it.

Salad Dressing

2 eggs
2 C. milk
6 T. flour
1 T. salt
2 t. dry mustard
1½ C. vinegar
1 C. sugar

Beat eggs in blender for a few minutes, then add milk, then dry ingredients. Add vinegar. Pour into top of double boiler and cook over boiling water until thickened, approx. 20 minutes. Pour into 1-quart jar and refrigerate.

Tomato Dressing

1 can tomato soup, condensed, 10 oz.
Dash of cayenne
¾ C. vinegar
5 T. brown sugar
1 t. onion, finely chopped
1 t. salt
½ t. pepper
1½ C. salad oil
1 t. dry mustard

Combine all ingredients in quart jar, shake vigorously, and chill. Shake again before serving.

Fruit Dressing

½ C. lemon juice
Dash cayenne
½ C. salad oil
3 T. white sugar
1 t. salt
1 T. maraschino cherries, finely chopped
½ t. paprika

Measure lemon juice and salad oil into a quart jar; add salt, paprika, and cayenne; add sugar. Shake well and chill. Just before serving, add maraschino cherries. This is great for fresh fruit salad.

German Potato Salad

10 med. potatoes cut to bite sizes
1 onion, chopped
1 stalk celery, diced
1 T. chopped parsley
3 hard cooked eggs, chopped
Mix together the above.
5 slices bacon, diced
½ cup cold water
2 eggs, well beaten
½ t. dry mustard
1 C. sugar
½ t. salt
½ C. vinegar
¼ t. pepper

Fry bacon in skillet until crisp and brown. Beat eggs, then add sugar, spices, vinegar, and water. Mix well and pour into the hot bacon fat, stir until mixture thickens (about 8 to 10 minutes). Pour over the potato mixture and mix lightly. Let stand in a cool place for several hours.

Three Bean Salad

1 C. sugar
2 t. salt
½ C. water, hot
5 T. salad oil
½ C. vinegar
Mix well, then add:
2 C. green beans
½ C. chopped celery
2 C. wax beans
½ C. chopped onions
2 C. kidney beans
Mix well and cool.

Remember: Smile at your neighbors all the time; it will drive them crazy!

Sour Milk Salad Dressing

½ C. water
½ C. vinegar
½ C. sugar
1 T. butter
1 t. salt
1 t. dry mustard
½ t. pepper
1 C. Carnation Milk
3 T. flour
2 eggs

Place vinegar, water, sugar, and butter in saucepan and let come to a boil. Beat together milk, flour, and eggs. Add to boiling mixture. Let boil for five minutes, stirring until it thickens, then just before removing from fire, add salt, mustard, and pepper, first mixing a little of the hot mixture until smooth.

Horseradish Sauce (for meats and fish)

4 T. butter
12 soda crackers, rolled fine
1 ¾ C. canned milk
¼ C. water
3 t. sugar
1/8 t. salt
1/8 t. paprika
3 T. horseradish

Melt butter in saucepan. Add cracker crumbs and stir until lightly yellow. Stir in milk very carefully. Add sugar, seasonings, and horseradish. Cook for about 2 to 3 minutes after all ingredients have been added. Makes 6 to 8 servings

Raisin Sauce, for Baked Ham

¾ C. raisins
1 C. water
5 cloves
¾ C. brown sugar
1 t. cornstarch
Dash of paprika
1 T. butter
1 T. vinegar
1 T. lemon juice
Few drops of Worcestershire sauce
1 t. horseradish

Cover raisins with water, add cloves, and allow to simmer until slightly thickened. Add butter and remaining ingredients. Serve hot.

WINE AND LIQUEUR

Grape Wine

1 basket of grapes 6 qt, mashed, skins and all left in enough hot water to make 1¼ gallons. Add 6 C. of sugar, 1½. pkg. yeast. Let stand for one week, then strain and squeeze all the juice out and bottle.

Beet Wine

7 lbs. beets peeled and cut up small. Boil in 1½ gallons water until soft. Strain and cool to lukewarm, then add:

   3 lbs. sugar
   1 lemon, sliced
   1 lb. raisins
   1 T. ginger

Mix well, then add 1 slice of toast, and sprinkle 1 pkg. yeast on top of toast. Let stand until fermenting stops. Strain and bottle but do not cap for another 2 days.

Dandelion Wine

2 qt. flowers only (no greens)
4 qt. boiling water
3 lbs. sugar
1 lbs. raisins
2 oranges, sliced
1 pkg. dry yeast

Mix flowers, sugar, fruit, and raisins. Pour in boiling water and let stand until lukewarm. Add dissolved yeast and let stand for two days. Strain and let stand until clear, then bottle.

Original Irish Cream

1 can Eagle Brand condensed milk
1 C. rye whiskey
2 eggs
½ pint whipping cream
3 T. chocolate syrup
1½ t. instant coffee

Put all ingredients in large bowl and mix well. Store in refrigerator.

Kahlua

3 C. sugar
10 T. instant coffee
Mix well, add:
3 1/3 C. of water

Bring to a boil and let simmer for ½ hour. Cool and skim. Then add 3 t. vanilla and 3 C. Vodka. Blend well and bottle.

Grand Marnier Liqueur

1 Mickey brandy
1 orange peel, grated
1 C. berry sugar

Heat until sugar dissolves. Let sit for 10 to 12 days, then strain and bottle.

Brandy Alexander Liqueur

1 300-ml. can sweetened condensed milk
½ C. cream de cacao
2 eggs
1 C. light cream
1 C. brandy
A pinch of nutmeg

Mix all ingredients together in a blender until smooth. Keep refrigerated and shake before serving. Sprinkle nutmeg on top of each drink before serving.

Spiced Maple Cider

½. gal. apple juice or cider
1 small orange, sliced
1 C. pure maple syrup
3 cinnamon sticks
1/3 C. of lemon juice
8 whole cloves
½ C. rum

In large saucepan combine all ingredients except rum; bring to a boil, reduce heat, and simmer uncovered for 20 minutes. Remove orange slices and spice. Add rum and serve warm. Garnish as desired. Can be served chilled, too. We add a bottle of ginger ale to make a punch.

A LITTLE HISTORY ABOUT ART

Working in the great Northwestern Ontario for many years as a guide and camp manager for fly-in camps with my family has given us the opportunity to begin our "back to the basics" lifestyle. Our family did not realize at the time that the biggest "catch" would not be found in any lakes, but would be found in an old trunk tucked away in the attic at our home in Kenora. Recipes dating back to the 30's belonging to the family. We have decided to share some of our treasures with special friends like you, friends who too want to get "back to the basics" and enjoy many years in the kitchen with your loved ones.

As far back as I can remember, my father would make Spiced Maple Cider, Apricot Liqueur, and Dandelion Wine. The Maple Cider and Apricot Liqueur he always made for Christmas. The Dandelion Wine was made every spring, and every spring we all picked dandelions. There were other things I would like to be doing in those days, but if you knew my father, you picked dandelions! After both my parents passed away, my brother and I found six one-gallon jugs of Dandelion Wine hidden in a closet. The dates on the jugs were 1965 to 1970. This wine was unbelievable; it was clear as water, smooth as silk, and kicked like a mule. We did treasure our find for many years. Thank you, Dad, for the great wine recipe.

MEAT RECIPES

It is not necessary to use wild game for some of the recipes below. Beef works just as well.

Moose in Beer Sauce

3 lbs. lean moose round roast
1 T. vinegar
3 T. corn oil
½ t. pepper
2 C. sliced onions
1/8 t. thyme
1¼ t. salt
1½ C. of beer
1 T. sugar

Cut moose meat into 2-inch cubes. Heat the oil in a heavy saucepan. Brown the onions and the moose meat in the oil. Add the salt, pepper, thyme, beer, sugar, and vinegar. Cover and cook over low heat for 1½ hours or until meat is tender.

Swiss Moose Steak

1½ lbs. lean moose steak, about 1 inch thick
Pepper to taste
2 T. beef fat
1 C. diced celery
½ C. diced onions
¼ C. flour
2 C. canned hot tomatoes

Mix flour with salt and pepper, and pound into both sides of steak with meat hammer. Sear steak on both sides in beef fat. Add celery, onions, and hot tomatoes. Cover and cook for two hours or until meat is tender. Add water as needed.

Moist Moose Roast

About a 3 lb. rump roast
1 large carrot, grated
Pinch of oregano
1 large onion, chopped fine
Pinch of rosemary
1 can of beef gravy

Grease a large sheet of heavy foil, place in roasting pan. Put the roast in center of foil and add all other ingredients. Wrap the foil securely over the roast; make sure it is leak proof and moisture will not escape. Roast in oven at 350°, 2½ to 3 hours or until done. Salt and pepper to taste. So much game is wasted because many people do not know how to cook it; they use the best cuts, and many times the rest is wasted.

Remember: It's a good idea to keep your words soft and sweet. You never know when you might have to eat them.

Sugar Cured Beef Steak

5 lbs. beef streak
1 t. saltpeter
5 t. sugar
1 t. pepper
5 t. salt

Mix well and sprinkle on both sides of meat, ring a cloth out of vinegar, and lay over meat. Let stand 8 to 10 days in a cool dry place. Fry and add one C. of beef broth to each quart, then boil for 2½ hours.

Brine for Smoking

Place meat, birds, or fish in crock pot and cover with:
    ½ lb. Morton's tender Quick salt
    3 T. liquid smoke
    4 T. sugar
    1 gallon water
Cover and let stand for 24 hours.

Baked Pork Chops

    4¼-inch pork chops
    Flour
    ½ C. ketchup
    5 t. brown sugar
    Pinch of dry mustard
Mix salt and pepper with flour, flour chops, and place in shallow dish. Mix ketchup, brown sugar, and dry mustard. Spread over each chop, add water to cover bottom of dish. Cover and bake for one hour at 350°. Remove cover and brown for 15 minutes. Salt and pepper to taste.

Remember: Old age is not of matter, but of the mind. If you don't mind, it doesn't matter.

Moose Stew (Kenora)

2 lbs. lean moose meat
½ t. pepper
2 T. cooking oil
¼ t. oregano
1 C. thinly sliced onions
1 C. dry wine
1 clove garlic, minced
1 T. tomato paste
1½ t. salt
½ C. boiling water

Cut meat into stew-sized pieces. Heat the oil in a Dutch oven or heavy saucepan; sauté the onions and garlic until soft. Add the meat and brown, and season with salt and pepper and oregano. Add the wine, tomato paste, and water. Bring to a boil, cover, and simmer on low heat, about 1½ hours or until done. If potatoes, carrots, or turnips are desired, then add 45 minutes before stew is done, and add more water if needed.

Dumplings for Stew

1½ C. flour
½ C. milk
1 t. salt
1 egg

Beat egg well, add salt and water, and stir into flour until smooth batter is formed. Drop by spoonful on top of stew, making sure they do not touch. Cover and cook until dumplings are done (3 to 5 minutes)

Moose in Sherry Sauce

3 lbs. lean moose round steak
1 T. vinegar
3 T. corn oil
½ t. pepper
1/8 t. thyme
2 C. sliced onions
1½ C. sherry
1½ t. salt
1 T. sugar

Cut moose into 2-inch cubes. Heat the oil in Dutch oven or heavy saucepan. Brown the onions and moose meat in it. Add the salt, pepper, thyme, beer, sugar, and vinegar. Cover and cook over low heat 1½ hours or until meat is tender.

Moose and Sausage Loaf

1 lb. finely ground moose meat
2 T. tomato ketchup
½ lbs. sausage meat
2 T. horseradish
1½ C. corn flake crumbs
½ t. prepared mustard
1 T. grated onion

½ C. milk

1 egg, slightly beaten

Thoroughly blend moose and sausage meat with crumbs, then add onion, ketchup, horseradish, mustard, and egg. Moisten with milk. Shape into loaf and bake in moderate oven at 350° for about one hour or until done.

Remember: The best helping hand you can find is at the end of your arm.

Art's Bear Stew

Cut meat into stew-sized pieces; rub with flour, which includes salt, pepper, garlic powder, a pinch of thyme, and a pinch of tarragon. Brown the meat thoroughly in heavy skillet in 3 T. cooking oil. Now add the following:

1½ C. sherry wine

½ C. of water

1 t. vinegar

Bring to a boil, cover, and simmer for about 2½ hours or until meat is tender. Add more wine and water if needed. 45 minutes before meat is done, add 4 cored and peeled apples, 4 carrots, cut, and 4 slices of onion.

Roast Venison

Venison loin roast (approx. 4 lbs.)
¼ t. marjoram
Salt and pepper
¼ t. thyme
Flour
½ C. water
4 T. beef fat
¼ C. wine

Mix salt and pepper, marjoram, thyme, and flour; rub this mix well into the meat, then sear on all sides in beef fat in heavy skillet. Place in roasting pan, add water and wine, cover and roast in oven at 325° for approximately 3 hours or until done to taste. Turn the roast often.

Venison Stew

About 2½ lbs. venison cut, stew-sized pieces
Pinch of oregano
2 onions, thinly sliced
¼ C. thinly sliced green pepper
Pinch of garlic powder
3 C. V8 Juice
1 bay leaf

Combine enough flour with salt and pepper to dredge the meat. Sear in bacon fat. Then add onions, garlic powder, bay leaf, green peppers, and V8 Juice. Cover and allow the meat to simmer for about 1 hour, or until meat is tender. Add more V8 Juice or water if necessary. Salt and pepper to taste.

Buffalo Steak

1 buffalo steak, about 1½ lbs. (or a 1-inch thick sirloin or round)

    1/3 C. flour
    1/8 t. pepper
    Garlic powder to taste
    Pinch of rosemary
    1 C. of sliced onions
    Pinch of thyme
    3 T. beef drippings
    ½ C. water
    1 t. salt
    ½ C. strained tomatoes
    ½ t. dry mustard

Cut the steak into serving pieces, and rub flour well into the meat. Sauté onions in 1 T. beef fat, in heavy skillet; remove. In same pan, sear steaks lightly on both sides in remaining beef fat. Blend together salt, mustard, pepper, garlic, rosemary, thyme, water, and tomatoes. Pour over steak and top with onions. Cover and cook over low heat about 1¼ hours or until meat is done to taste.

Canadian Pea-meal Bacon

5 lbs. pork loin
2½. T. salt
2 T. sugar
1 t. Cure # 1
1 qt. ice water

Dissolve all ingredients in water and chill to 38°. With a spray pump inject the loin with some of the curing. Put in plastic bag or container and add the remaining pickling cure. Place in refrigerator at 38° for 4 to 5 days. Remove and wash loin in cold water, let dry for one hour. Rub loin with coarse corn meal, refrigerate.

Swiss Moose Steak

From a 2 lb. moose round cut ¼-inch slices, rub with salt and pepper.

1 T. sugar
1 large can tomatoes
1 bay leaf
4 t. cornmeal
1 onion, sliced
1 clove garlic
1 T. soy sauce
3 stalks celery, cut
½ t. thyme

Brown meat with onions, garlic in oil, then sprinkle

with sugar. Add 1 can of consommé, bay leaf, thyme, soy sauce, and celery. Cook slowly for two hours, well covered. Then add tomatoes, and cook uncovered in oven for one hour at 350° or until meat is tender. Add water or tomato juice if necessary. Thicken juice with 4 t. cornmeal and a little cold water.

Moose Sausage and Beer Loaf

1 lb. ground moose meat
½ lb. ground sausage meat
1½ C. corn flake crumbs
1 T. onion powder
2 T. ketchup
2 T. horseradish
1 egg, slightly beaten
½ C. beer
½ t. prepared mustard

Mix well the moose, sausage, and corn flake crumbs. Add onion, ketchup, horseradish, mustard, and egg. Moisten with beer. Shape into loaf and bake in moderate oven at 350° for about one hour, or until done.

Art's Moose Stew

1 lb. moose meat, cubed
1 C. sliced carrots
¼ C. beef drippings
2 potatoes, cut up
½ t. salt
1 onion, copped
½ t. pepper
½ can tomato soup
½ C. water

Heat beef drippings in heavy skillet, and sear meat, add onion, salt, pepper, and half the water. Bring to a boil, then lower heat and simmer for about 30 minutes. Add carrots, potatoes, tomato soup, and ½ C. of water. Cook until vegetables are tender; add more water if necessary.

SMALL GAME AND BIRDS

Sautéed Frog's Legs

Several frog legs
1 T. grated onion
Flour
½ t. salt and pepper to taste
1 t. lemon juice

Mix salt and pepper with enough flour to dredge the frog's legs. Sauté the onions with butter in fry pan, then add frog legs and lemon juice. Stir and cook over low heat 10 to 15 minutes. They should be brown and tender.

Rabbit Stew
(you can use squirrel for this too)

2 rabbits, cut into serving pieces
½ C. chopped celery
½ C. butter
½ t. oregano
3 T. flour
2 onions, cut
1 t. salt
4 carrots, cut
¼ t. pepper
6 potatoes, cut
3 C. water

Combine flour, salt, and pepper, and dredge rabbit in this mix. Brown rabbit in fry pan then add water, oregano, celery, onions, carrots, and potatoes. Cover and cook 1 hour. Blend 3 T. flour in 3 T. butter until golden brown, then add this to the stew and cook for 10 minutes.

Buttered Fried Rabbit

2 rabbits
¼ t. oregano
4 T. flour
¼ t. basil
2 t. salt
½ t. pepper

10 T. butter

5 T. hot water

Cut rabbit for frying. Combine flour, salt, pepper, basil, and oregano, and dredge rabbit with this mix. Brown on all sides in butter in covered skillet; then add 5 T. hot water. Cover and let simmer for 45 minutes, or until tender. Make gravy from remaining liquid.

Baked Partridge in Sherry

2 med.-sized partridges

¼ t. pepper

1 small clove of garlic, chopped

1 t. salt

1 small onion, chopped

1/3 C. butter

¼ C. chopped celery

½ C. sherry wine

Cut up birds using breasts and thighs. Brown lightly, with butter, garlic, and onion. Turn into roasting pan, add sherry wine and chopped celery. Bake 1½ hours covered in moderate oven. Baste frequently to prevent dryness. Add a little water as it's roasting to increase gravy.

Roast Duck (Mallard)

1 duck, about 3 lbs., cleaned well
1 med. apple, quartered
½ t. salt
1 small onion, quartered
¼ t. pepper
1 celery stalk, chopped
1 T. butter
½ C. hot water
2 T. poultry seasoning
1 T. vinegar

Rub duck inside and out with salt and pepper and poultry seasoning. Place apple, onion, and celery inside duck. Place duck in roaster breast down, melt butter in hot water, add vinegar, and pour over duck. Cover and place in hot oven for 20 minutes. Reduce heat to 300° and cook until tender, about 2 hours. Season gravy, lightly.

Art's Wild Duck

Cut off breasts and cut up remainder, as you would chicken for frying. Salt and pepper, then roll in flour. Fry in butter until golden brown, turning frequently. Pour off butter and place duck in covered saucepan and cover entirely with equal parts of ginger ale, orange juice, and 2 T. brandy (mix well). Pour over duck and cook over low heat until tender. Add more juice from time to time, it evaporates quickly.

Basting For Wild Duck or Goose

½ C. of port wine
½ C. of currant jelly
3 T. prepared mustard
¼ C. water

Put all ingredients in saucepan, bring to a boil while stirring. Use this to baste bird. When bird is finished, mix sauce with drippings in pan and serve with the bird. Salt and pepper to taste.

Roast Wild Goose

1 goose, prepared for roasting
1 T. vinegar
Salt and pepper
1 onion
Flour

Season goose inside and out with vinegar, then salt and pepper. Place the onion in the cavity and let stand overnight. Remove onion, dredge with flour, then place in roasting pan in slow oven at 325°. Roast uncovered until tender and brown, 20 to 25 minutes per pound. Keep basting with the juices from the pan.

Stuffing for Wild Goose

1 quart dry bread, diced
1 t. salt
Liver, heart, and gizzard, chopped fine
1/8 t. pepper
¼ onion copped fine
¼ t. ginger
¼ C. celery diced
1/8 t. nutmeg
½ C. strained tomatoes
1 egg
2 T. fat

Soak the bread in water and squeeze dry. Heat the fat in skillet. Add bread and fry. Add other ingredients, and mix well.

SAUSAGE MAKING AND PICKLING

The recipes on this page are our family's favorites. Try the spiced tomatoes on steaks.

Spiced Tomatoes

4 lbs. ripe tomatoes
2 lbs. brown sugar
1 pint vinegar
½ t. cloves
½ t. cinnamon

Stew until thick as molasses. Cool before putting in jars.

Dresden Pickles

12 large cucumbers, peeled
6 onions
5 heads celery
5 green peppers
5 red peppers

Remove seeds from peppers and cut celery into medium pieces. Put all through a food chopper and sprinkle with salt. Let stand overnight. Drain and add:

3 pints vinegar
1½ lbs. brown sugar
2 T. celery seed
3 T. mustard seed.

Mix well and put in jars. *No* cooking.

If you have never tasted Dresden Pickles, then you're in for a treat.

Pickled Prunes

Soak 1 lb. prunes overnight in cold water. Boil 5 minutes in same water. Drain. Pour over 1 C. vinegar, ½ C. brown sugar, 1 t. whole cloves, and 1 t. cinnamon. Boil 5 minutes longer and seal in jars while hot.

Tomato Juice

1 eleven-quart basket tomatoes, washed and cut up. Boil with 7 t. salt, ½ C. sugar, 3 onions, celery tops, or 1 t. pepper if desired. Boil for two hours, strain, and bottle.

Dill Carrots

Cook whole small carrots, about 10 minutes. Do not cook till soft. Add dill to sterile jars and arrange carrots. Pour over the following syrup:

3 C. sugar
3 C. vinegar
1½ C. water
Cucumber Relish
6 large cucumbers
1 bunch celery
1 lb. onions

Put all through chopper, cover with salt and water. Let stand for 2 hours, then drain. Mix:

2 t. mustard
1 t. turmeric
½ t. cayenne pepper
2 ½ C. sugar
1 pint vinegar
3 T. flour

Pour over cucumbers and bring to a boil. Put into jars and seal.

Homemade Pickles

At one time experts taught us that pickles thinned the blood and were health diminishing instead of health promoting. This view has changed. Green pickles particularly retain their vitamin content. Used judiciously, they titillate a jaded appetite, spark up a dull meal, and make a conversation piece if artistically displayed. Relish dishes divided into compartments make an ideal service piece for your best and most decorative pickles.

Garlic Sausage

15 lbs. beef
15 lbs. pork
½ C. salt
½ C. saltpeter
2 T. pepper
3 ½ C. water
6 cloves garlic, crushed
2 T. paprika

Grind all meats and mix well. Add remaining ingredients, mix well, and let stand overnight, covered. Fill casings and smoke or bake in oven for one hour at 300°. Prick sausage first before cooking.

Polish Sausage

4 lbs. beef, trimmed
1 lb. beef fat
1½ lbs. lean pork
2 t. pepper
3 t. marjoram
3 t. garlic powder
1 t. cayenne pepper

Grind meats separately, mix together well, and grind again, then sprinkle all the seasonings on all the meat, mix well, and grind a third time. Stuff into casings, place in a cake pan, and cover with water. Bake at 350° until all the water has evaporated. Wrap and freeze.

Homemade Salami

4 lbs. ground beef
1 T. Liquid Smoke
1 T. garlic powder
1 C. water
1 T. onion salt
1 T. mustard seed
4 lbs. Morton's tender quick salt
1 T. pepper

Mix all ingredients well and form into 3 rolls, wrap in foil with shiny side in. Refrigerate for 24 hours. Poke holes in bottom of each roll and place on oven rack, place a pan of water under rolls, and bake for 90 minutes at 300°. Cool and wrap in plastic to store, freeze well.

The Homemade Salami recipe has been in our family for years. I make this recipe every month. The best salami I have made is made with moose and venison, but you must add a little beef fat, or it will be dry. I also like this recipe because of how easy it is; you don't need to stuff casings.

Beef Jerky

    1 lb. round steak
    1 t. salt
    ½ t. garlic salt
    ¼ t. pepper
    ¼ t. Liquid Smoke

Cut partially frozen steak into 1/8 strips. Wipe strips with Liquid Smoke. Mix spices, then sprinkle on both sides of strips. Bake in oven for 8 to 10 hours at 180°.

Perfect Sweet Pickles

Wash small cucumbers, onions, and cauliflower. Pack in quart sealers with 1 T. of salt to each, fill with cold water, shake well, and let stand for two hours. Pour off and mix 2 quarts cider vinegar, 1 qt. water, ¼ C. salt, 1 heaping t. mixed spices, 1 t. saccharin powder, and 1 t. celery seed. Seal and shake.

Oil Pickles

This recipe is for a 1-gallon crock pot. Soak cucumbers for 3 days in brine. Add cauliflower and onions to hot brine and let sit overnight. Boil 1 gallon of vinegar, 8 lbs. sugar, and 1 T. alum for five minutes. Turn off, and add onions and cauliflowers. Let stand overnight. Next, stir in 4 T. pickle oil, and stir every day. No sealing. Pickles can be left in crock.

Bread and Butter Pickles

24 medium cucumbers, sliced ¼ inch thick. Let stand in a strong solution of salt and water overnight. Drain. Mix:

    1 ½ pts. vinegar
    1 t. turmeric
    2 t. ginger
    2 t. mustard seed
    2 t. celery seed
    4 C. sugar

Boil and add cucumbers for five minutes, bottle, and seal.

Dill Pickles

Wash and wipe dry cucumbers and pack into sterile jars with plenty of dill. Heat until boiling.

1 C. vinegar
1 C. water
1 t. salt

For each jar and pour over cucumbers. Boil tops and lids, then seal jars.

Pickled Fish

Cut fish into bite-sized pieces. Make a brine of 1 qt. vinegar and ¾ C. coarse pickling salt. Add fish. Let stand for five days in the refrigerator, stirring every day. On the fifth day, rinse in cold water. Make a solution of:

2 C. vinegar
1 C. sugar
1 t. ginger
1½ T. pickling oil
1½ t. hickory liquid smoke

Bring to a boil then let cool. Pack a layer of fish and a layer of onions to fill jar. Pour cooled solution over fish and onions, seal jars, and let stand for one week.

Pickled Eggs

2 dozen hard-boiled eggs.
Chill, then make a solution of
2½ C. vinegar
4 T. sugar
2 t. salt
2½ C. cold water
3 t. pickling spices in a bag

Mix and boil for 10 minutes. When cool, pour over eggs and let stand for one week. This recipe can be used for sausage, too.

Remember: Keep your eyes wide open before marriage and half closed afterwards.

per. Cook over low heat until thickened, stirring constantly. Add fish and serve on toast.

Fried Catfish

6 catfish, skinned and cleaned

½ C. canned milk

8 T. bacon fat

Salt and pepper to taste

½ C. cornmeal

1/8 t. thyme

Pinch of rosemary

Sprinkle the fish inside with salt and pepper. Dip fish in the milk, then in the cornmeal. Melt bacon in skillet quite hot, but don't allow to smoke. Fry fish on one side until golden brown, then season by sprinkling with the thyme and rosemary. Turn carefully. Fry the other side for five minutes, until fish flakes easily. Serve with lemon juice.

Catfish Stew (This is delicious)

Several catfish, skinned and cleaned, bring them to a boil in salted water for 5 to 7 minutes. Pour off water and separate fish from bones. Cut fish into stew-sized pieces; put fish into a large saucepan and add the following ingredients:

3 C. water
Salt and pepper to taste
2 T. chopped celery
2 finely diced potatoes
2 T. chopped onion
1 chopped carrot
3 T. butter
Pinch of marjoram
4 C. milk
Pinch of sage

Deep Fry Fish Cheeks

Fish cheeks are boneless, skinless, and are quite a delicacy. Wash well, and beat 2 eggs with salt and pepper. Dip cheeks in egg mix, then roll in 2 C. of corn flake crumbs. Deep fry at medium heat in your favorite oil. Cook until golden brown.

Fried Fish Livers

If you caught several large fish, such as bass, trout, whitefish, walleye, or pike, etc., remove the livers. Toll the livers in flour seasoned with salt and pepper. Fry in shallow fat until done.

Court Bouillon

No wild game cookbook would be complete without a recipe for Court Bouillon. Court Bouillon has been handed down for several generations. From France it journeyed to Louisiana and is now used in almost in every country in the world. There are many variations.

Court Bouillon

1 ½ T. fat
3 cloves
1 ½ T. flour
¼ t. thyme
1 lb. sliced fish
2 bay leaves
2 C. tomatoes
4 C. water
3 T. lemon juice
1 t. salt
1 green pepper, chopped
½ t. pepper
1 small onion, chopped
½ t. cayenne
½ clove garlic, minced
5 drops Tabasco sauce

Melt fat, add flour, and brown lightly. Add remaining ingredients and simmer for 45 minutes.

Scrambled Salmon

This is one of my oldest recipes. Try this recipe on your next camping trip.

    1 large canned pink salmon, well drained
    7 or 8 eggs
    10 to 12 slices bacon

Fry bacon in skillet, remove bacon, and dispose of most of the grease. Put salmon in skillet and stir until heated and broken fine. Break in the eggs and scramble all until eggs are cooked to taste. Season with salt and pepper and serve with bacon.

Milk Baked Trout

    5 lbs. trout, cleaned
    1 C. milk
    Salt and pepper
    5 T. butter
    1 T. lemon juice

Rub fish inside and out with salt, and dust with pepper. Place fish in pan and add milk. Bake for one hour at 325° or until fish flakes. Remove fish to a platter; don't break the fish. Remove skin and bones. Melt the butter and lemon juice and pour over the fish and serve.

Beer Batter for Fish

1 C. flour
1 t. baking powder
1 egg
1 C. beer
1 small can condescend milk
Flour

Mix in mixer for about one minute, pour into bowl, and add flour and mix well until thickens. Dip fish and deep fry until golden brown.

The next recipe, for fish chowder, was made one day every week for many years at the camp. Our customers would always ask for this recipe, to take home with them. If you like fish chowder, then you will love this one. This recipe was given to me many years ago, by the head chef at the Red Lion Inn on Bimini Island, in the Bahamas.

Bimini Fish Chowder

About 2 lbs. fish, cubed
3 large carrots, diced
5 strips bacon, chopped
4 C. boiling water
3 T. butter
1 T. salt
½ T. pepper
1 medium onion, chopped
1 C. celery, diced
1 can condensed milk
3 raw potatoes, diced
1 t. garlic salt

Melt butter in saucepan and cook onions, celery, and bacon until tender. Then put into large pot and add potatoes, carrots, water, salt, and pepper. Cover and simmer for about 20 minutes, until vegetables are tender. Add fish and cook for 10 more minutes. Remove from heat and add milk, mix well. Now here is the best part of this fish chowder. To each hot bowl of fish chowder served, add 1 T. of white wine, stir, and serve.

I worked and fished for many years in the Bahaman Islands, and it was there that I found many great recipes, and I have found that most of the recipes work well with freshwater fish.

CANDIES AND JAMS

Taffy Apples

Syrup
1 C. sugar
1/3 C. corn syrup
2/3 C. water
1 t. vanilla

Boil to a hard ball stage, 250° in cold water. Put skewer in middle of apple and dip in syrup. Stand on greased pan.

Mints

1 lb. icing sugar
1 T. butter
1 drop of peppermint oil
1 dash cream of tartar

Dampen with hot water. Roll into balls then pat with fork into patties.

Sea Foam

3 C. sugar
2/3 C. water
½ C. corn syrup

Boil until soft ball forms in water. Beat the white of 2 eggs stiff, and add ½ t. salt. Next pour the above mix slowly over whites of eggs, beating all the while. Continue until very stiff. Add chopped nuts and turn into greased pan. Cut into squares when cold.

Chocolate Covered Cherries

1 bottle cherries
1 egg white
1 t. almond flavoring
1 lb. icing sugar
2 squares sweet chocolate
1 small piece paraffin wax

Beat egg whites stiff. Add water and flavoring. Add

icing sugar until you can form into firm balls. Roll mixture around each cherry to form a ball. Place on wax paper in cool place for two hours. Place chocolate and wax in saucepan over boiling water. Spear each ball with toothpick and dip into chocolate mix and let cool.

Peach Conserve

5 C. peaches, peeled, stoned, and cubed
2 T. lemon juice
1 med. orange, thinly sliced
2 C. sugar
1 C. corn syrup
¼ C. drained quartered maraschino cherries
Cook until thick, place in jars.

Orange Marmalade

Remove seeds from 7 med. oranges, 1 med. lemon, and 1 med. grapefruit. Put pulp and rind through grinder. Add 16 C. of water and boil until tender. Add 16 C. of sugar and cook until thick as desired low heat.

Strawberry Jam

4 C. strawberries, mashed
5 C. sugar
1 pkg. powdered pectin
1 C. water
Add sugar to strawberries, mix well, and let stand for

half hour. Stir now and then. Dissolve pectin in water and boil for one minute. Add hot pectin to strawberries and stir for a few minutes. Cover and let stand for 48 hours, or until it has jelled. Store in the refrigerator or freeze it.

Pear Jam

5 C. ripe pears, crushed
5 C. of sugar
20 oz. can crushed pineapple
1 pkg. lemon Jell-O
1 pkg. orange Jell-O

Mix pears and sugar, boil for five minutes, then add crushed pineapple. Bring to a boil then remove from heat, add both Jell-Os, and stir well until dissolved. Bottle and seal.

Tropical Jam

10 peaches
8 pears
6 apples
3 oranges
2 lemons
6 lbs. sugar
½ C. chopped maraschino cherries

Cut and remove seeds from all fruit. Run oranges and lemons through grinder, rinds and all. Mix all together and add 6 lbs. sugar. Mix well and let stand overnight. Next day, boil for one hour, then put in jars and seal.

Rhubarb Marmalade

10 lbs. rhubarb
10 lbs. sugar
10 oranges
2 lemons

Wash and cut rhubarb into 1-inch pieces. Add sugar and the juice and ground rinds of the fruits. Boil until thick, about 20 to 30 minutes. Pour into hot sterilized jars and seal.

Apple Butter

2 gallons apples
Cinnamon
5 lbs. sugar

Wash and cut up apples, add 5 lbs. sugar, and let stand overnight. Next day, bring to a boil for 2 hours (covered). Strain and add cinnamon to taste.

Canned Blueberries

6 quarts blueberries
2 C. water
5 C. sugar
1 T. limejuice
¼ salt

Wash and pick over blueberries; put in kettle with water and salt. Cover and cook for 10 minutes with low heat, then add limejuice and sugar and bring to a boil. Simmer for 3 to 4 minutes. Pour overflowing into sterile jars and seal.

Canned Peaches (in your oven)

6 qt. peaches
3 lbs. sugar
3 C. water
1 drop of red food coloring

Scald and skin peaches; cut in half, but leave pits in mixture. Mix all together and simmer on low for five minutes. Remove pits and pack into sterile jars within ¼ inch from top. Adjust lids, screw down tightly, then loosen lids back ¼ turn. Place jars on oven rack and bake 35 minutes (pints) or 45 minutes (quarts) at 275°. Remove jars from oven; tighten lids and invert jars for 24 hours.

Plum Jam

8 C. chopped prune plums
6 C. sugar
1 C. water
1 t. Epsom salts

Wash, pit, and chop plums into small pieces. Measure fruit (tightly packed) and add water into kettle. Simmer for 15 minutes. Add sugar, mix well, and bring to rolling boil for one minute. Remove from heat; stir in Epsom salts. Boil again until it thickens (about 20 minutes). Pour into sterile jars. Cover with hot wax.

COOKIES AND TARTS

Old Fashioned Gingersnaps

1/3 C. margarine
2 t. hot water
¾ C. sugar
2 ½ C. sifted cake flour
1 egg, well beaten
½ t. cinnamon
½ C. molasses
½ t. ginger
2 t. baking soda

Cream together margarine and sugar; beat until light. Add well-beaten egg and molasses. Dissolve baking soda in hot water and add to creamed mixture. Add sifted dry ingredients; blend well. Chill batter for two hours. Roll out on a lightly floured board; cut with 2-inch floured cutter. Bake at 350° for about 12 to 15 minutes on an oiled cookie sheet.

Old-Fashioned Sugar Cookies

1/3 C. shortening
1/8 t. baking soda
1 C. sugar
½ t. salt
1 egg, unbeaten
¼ C. sour cream or milk
2 C. sifted cake flour
2 t. pure vanilla extract

Cream together shortening and sugar until it is like ice cream. Add eggs; beat until light and creamy. Sift flour three times; add alternately with sour milk to cream batter. Add vanilla, mix well, then cool batter for three hours. Drop by spoonfuls on oiled cookies sheet and bake at 350° in moderate oven until done (about 12 to 15 minutes).

Nut and Raisin Cookies

1 C. brown sugar
½ C. shortening
1 egg
1 C. milk
1 t. molasses

2 C. flour
3 t. baking powder
1 t. cloves and mace
1 C. raisins
½ C. chopped nuts

Blend well and drop on buttered cookie sheet. When out of oven, sprinkle with sugar. Bake at 350° until golden brown.

Coffee Cookies

3 C. brown sugar
4 t. baking powder
1½ C. lard
A few drops of vanilla and lemon
1 ½ C. coffee
4 eggs
1 ½ t. soda
6 C. flour

Mix coffee and flour first, then mix all other ingredients. Drop onto cookie sheet. Bake at 350° until light brown.

Soft Molasses Cookies

1 C. shortening
2 t. ginger
1 C. sugar
2 t. cinnamon
1 C. molasses
½ t. cloves
1 C. sour cream
½ t. nutmeg
6 C. flour
1 t. salt
3 t. soda

Cream shortening and sugar. Add molasses. Sift flour, spices, and salt. Add alternately with sour cream to form soft dough. Chill in refrigerator overnight. Roll out to ½ inch thick, cut, and put raisins in the center of each cookie. Bake in oven at 350° for 6 to 8 minutes. You can put on any icing on you like.

Sour Cream Cookies

1 C. brown sugar
1 t. salt
1 C. white sugar
4 t. baking powder
1 C. shortening
4 ½ C. flour

Gentlemen, the Tartan
Here's to it.
The fighting sheen of it,
The yellow, the green of it,
The white, the blue of it,
The swing, the hue of it,
The dark, the red of it,
Every thread of it!
The fair have sighed for it,
The brave have died for it,
Foemen sought for it,
Heroes fought for it.
Honor the name of it,
Drink to the fame of it
The Tartan.

VITAMINS AND MINERALS

Vitamins and minerals have become part of daily life, but not so many of us realize that, for health, vitamins and minerals should go hand in hand. Following is a guide to the uses of vitamins and minerals in daily menu building.

Vitamin	Use in Body	Best Sources
A	For normal vision	Leafy greens, yellow vegetables and fruits
B1 (Thiamin)	For good appetite, good digestion and steady nerves	Enriched and whole grain bread and cerial, Dried peas, beans, peanuts, pork and liver
C (Asorbic Acid)	Healthy teeth, gums, bones and blood vessels	Citrus fruits, tomato juice, leafy greens and potato
D	For normal development of teeth and bones	Salmon, sardines, mackerel, fish liver oils, milk and egg yolk
G (Riboflavin)	For healthy skin and eyes	Liver, kidney, lean beef, leafy greens, milk

Niacin (Nicotinic Acid)	For healthy skin	Whole grain bread and cereals, liver and lean meats
Iron	For healthy red blood cells	Dried fruits, liver and lean meats, dried peas or beans, whole grain cereals, green vegetables, molasses, and egg
Calcium	For strong bones and teeth	Cheese, milk, leafy greens
Phosphorus	For development of healthy bones and teeth	Meat, fish, dried peas, and beans

INTERNATIONAL DISHES

Scotch Short Bread

4 C. flour
½ C. sugar
1 C. butter

Cream butter well. Add sugar. Work in sifted flour. When mixture is too stiff to mix with spoon, turn on pastry board and rub in the remaining flour. Roll ¾ inch thick. Spread in well-oiled baking sheet. Bake in hot oven (400°) for five minutes, then at 350° for about 25 minutes longer. It should be a very pale brown. Cut into wedges to serve.

Bohemian Potato Dumplings

Boil 3 to 4 medium-sized potatoes and put through ricer. Cool. Add:

2 T. farina
1 egg
1 t. salt

Mix thoroughly. Add enough flour to make a stiff dough. Form into a roll and cut into pieces about 1 to 1½ inches thick, rolling into balls and dropping into boiling water; cook about 8 minutes. Remove from water and drain. Serve on hot platter with melted butter.

Crepes Suzette (French Pancakes)

½ C. flour
1 t. baking powder
¼ t. salt
2 T. melted butter
1 egg
½ C. Carnation Milk, diluted with
½ C. water

Heat milk. Sift flour, baking powder, and salt together. Beat egg lightly. Add hot milk and melted butter. When slightly cooled, stir into sifted dry ingredients. Beat until perfectly smooth, using rotary beater. Heat griddle and grease. Pour batter into skillet to form a

3-inch pancake. Turn with spatula as soon as it is light brown. Any sauce or jam will do.

Norwegian Frukt Suppe (Fruit Soup)

Cook ½ C. pear tapioca in 3 C. water until transparent. Then add ½ C. cooked raisins, ½ C. cooked pitted prunes, juice of 1 lemon, and sugar to taste. Simmer low for 3 to 4 minutes. Serve hot or cold.

Chinese Eggs

½ C. uncooked rice
4 hard-cooked eggs
2 T. finely minced green pepper
1 t. minced onion
2 T. tomato puree
¼ C. ground cooked ham
¼ lb. soft cheese
¾ C. Carnation Milk
Pinch of paprika

Cook the rice in boiling salted water until tender. Rinse, drain, and arrange in a buttered baking dish. Cut the hard-cooked eggs in half lengthwise, remove, then mash, then mix with green peppers, onion, tomato puree, and ground ham. Season to taste with salt and paprika and work to a paste. Fill the egg whites and press into the egg rice. Dissolve the cheese in the milk and pour over the eggs and rice. Place in moderate oven

(350°) for 25 minutes. Let stand in warm place about 20 minutes before serving. Salt to taste.

Danish Kleine

These cookies are really little fried cakes, a traditional Danish Cake.

2 egg yolks
½ C. sugar
½ C. milk
½ C. cooking oil
2 eggs
1 t. baking powder
½ t. almond extract
Flour

Beat eggs and egg yolks, add sugar, and beat with a spoon for 10 minutes. Add oil, milk, extract, and 1 C. flour sifted with baking powder. Add more flour to make a stiff dough. Roll out and cut dough into diamonds about 2 inches long with a slit in the middle. Pass one end of diamond through this slit and drop cake in hot, deep fat. Fry a light brown, drain, and dust with powdered sugar.

Strawberry Things

Fresh strawberries work the best. Spear a cleaned straw-berry with a toothpick. Dip the strawberry in a glass of Grand Marnier Liqueur for the count of five. Then roll it in a dish of powdered sugar and serve. We make this recipe every year at Christmas.

Scandinavian Potatoes

- 6 medium potatoes
- 6 anchovies
- ½ t. chopped parsley
- ½ t. dry mustard
- 2 T. butter
- 2 egg yolks

Pare the potatoes, cook in salted water until tender, then put through the ricer. Add the anchovies, drained from oil, and cut in ¼-inch pieces. Add the chopped parsley, dry mustard, butter, and seasonings. Blend thoroughly and stir in the beaten egg yolks. Cook three minutes, stirring constantly. Remove from heat, pour into a shallow baking dish, and let cool. Mold in the form of small eggs, roll in breadcrumbs, then in beaten egg, then in breadcrumbs again. Fry in deep hot fat. Garnish with parsley. Salt and pepper to taste.

Swedish Meat Balls

¾ lbs. ground beef
¼ lb. veal
¼ lb. lean pork
½ t. pepper
2 T. onion
1 ½ C. milk
2 eggs
½ C. breadcrumbs
2 t. salt
½ T. butter

Grind meats three times. Beat milk and eggs together and pour over breadcrumbs. After well mixed, combine with meat. Add seasonings and onion, which have been fried. Form into small balls and brown in butter. Add a little hot water and simmer 10 minutes.

Polish Salad

Remove the outer leaves from 2 heads of lettuce. Cut each into quarters and arrange on plates. Make the following dressing: 2 hard-cooked eggs. Take the yolk of 1 egg and mash. Mix with ½ t. sugar, 1 C. milk, 1 T. lemon juice, and a dash of salt. Mix thoroughly and pour over lettuce. Dice the other egg and the white of the first egg and scatter over the salad.

Spanish Fried Chicken

1 chicken, cut up for frying
4 T. cooking fat
1 chopped onion
1 chopped green pepper
1 C. chopped tomatoes
½ T. chili powder
½ C. rice, uncooked
1 C. milk

Cook onions in fat for a few minutes; roll chicken in flour and brown on both sides. Add other ingredients and enough water to cook rice. Cook slowly, covered, in oven, until chicken is tender. If necessary add more milk to cook rice, as it must be quite dry when served.

Hungarian Stuffed Cabbage

Take one head of soft cabbage; remove leaves separately and put in saltwater overnight. Take 1 lb. ground pork, put in dish, and add:

1 C. cooked rice
2 raw eggs
½ onion, finely chopped
Salt and pepper
½ C. milk
½ T. lemon juice

Mix all well together and put two heaping tablespoons

in each cabbage leaf; roll it, then cook the rolls of stuffed cabbage in 1 lb. of sauerkraut and necessary water for about two hours.

Russian Borscht

1 or 2 beef shanks, covered with water. Add:
¼ C. barley
1 large minced onion
Celery leaves

Cook until the meat is very tender. Remove the bones and cut into smaller pieces. Put back in pot and add salt and pepper to taste. Add 4 diced fresh beets with tops. If tops are unavailable, use spinach. Add 3 diced carrots and plenty of fresh dill. Serve with sour cream and hot rolls.

Remember: You cannot do a kindness too soon; you never know how soon it will be too late.

Lefse

Combine gradually, and blend thoroughly:
2 C. flour
½ C. melted butter
2 C. mashed potatoes
½ t. salt

Mix to a smooth dough. Roll out very thin in rounds to fit your skillet. Cook quickly on both sides on lightly greased skillet until golden brown.

We enjoy these spread with plum jam and a few drops of maple syrup.

Trinidad Curried Chicken

1 C. Chicken
1 onion, chopped
1 can tomato soup
3 cloves
1 t. cumin seed
2 pepper corns
1 stick cinnamon
2 T. brown sugar
2 T. oil
1 t. curry powder
2 T. salt
1 t. turmeric
1 t. water
1 t. lemon juice

Heat oil in large pot. Add cumin seeds, turmeric, and onions, and cook until onions are dark brown. Add tomatoes and spices and cook until you can see the colors. Add chicken and cook until chicken is done. Before serving, add water, lemon juice, and curry powder. Mix well.

To Make a Garlic Salad

Try this next time you make a salad. In large salad bowl place 1 T. salt and 2 cloves of garlic. With a spoon, mash garlic into salt until it becomes a paste, and smear over sides of all the bowl. Add your vegetables and mix well, then serve.

ART'S FAVORITE RECIPES

Art's Old Canadian Pancakes

2 C. Flour
6 t. baking powder
1½ t. salt
¼ C. sugar
¼ C. vegetable oil
1 ¾. C. milk (buttermilk is very good, too)
2 eggs, beaten
Mix well, fry on hot griddle.

Bush Syrup

Boil 6 potatoes in 4 C. of water until 1 C. of water is left in the pot. In the 1 C. of water, dissolve 1 C. of white sugar and 1 C. of brown sugar. Put mixture in jar with lid and let stand at room temperature for one week. Chill and serve.

Butterscotch Sauce

1 C. brown sugar
1 T. vinegar
1/8 t. salt
4 T. butter
½ C. cold water
½ t. vanilla

Cook sugar, butter, vinegar, water, and salt, stirring frequently until a soft ball will form in cold water. Add the vanilla and serve over ice cream. This sauce can be reheated just before serving.

Hot Fudge Sauce for Ice Cream

6 T. margarine
1 (13 oz.) can evaporated milk
1 C. sugar
1 t. vanilla
6 T. cocoa

Mix together margarine, sugar, and cocoa in saucepan. Cook over medium heat until butter is completely melted. Remove from heat and add vanilla. Serve hot or cold. Makes about 2 C.

Apple Butter

2 gal. apples, cut up
5 lbs. white sugar

Mix and let stand overnight. Next morning, boil for three hours (covered). Strain if you have to. Then add cinnamon to taste.

Pancake Syrup

2 ¼ C. sugar
1 t. Mapeline
¼ C. brown sugar
1 ½ C. hot water

Mix until sugar is dissolved. Makes approximately 1 ½ pt.

Honey Vinegar

Mix together in a crock one quart of honey and eight quarts of water. Allow the mixture to stand in a warm place until fermentation ceases. The resulting vinegar is white and excellent. Put in jars and seal.

Eggnog

4 eggs
1/8 t. nutmeg
4 C. milk
1/8 t. salt
4 T. lemon juice
1/3 C. sugar
½ C. cream

Beat eggs until thick and lemon colored. Add sugar, salt, nutmeg, and lemon juice. Add ice-cold milk and cream. Beat until frothy. Makes about 6 large glasses.

TABLE OF MEASUREMENTS

The essential tools for a good cook are a good sifter, a standard measuring cup, and standard measuring spoons. Here are four simple rules for success in baking.

1.   Sift all flour before measuring.

2.   When filling cups with liquids, place cup on table so that measure is accurate.

3.   Have shortening at room temperature so that it may be accurately and easily packed in cup.

4.   All measurements are level.

Table of Measurements

Dash	less than 1/8 teaspoon
3 teaspoons	1 tablespoon
4 tablespoons	¼ cup
5 tablespoons+1 teaspoon	1/3 cup
8 tablespoons	½ cup
10 tablespoons+2 teaspoons	2/3 cup
12 tablespoons	¾ cup
16 tablespoons	1 cup
4 cups or 2 pints	1 quart
16 cups or 4 quarts	1 gallon
2 gallons or 8 quarts	1 peck
4 pecks	1 bushel
16 ounces (dry measure)	1 pound

Every man should eat, drink, and enjoy the fruit of his labor; it is the gift of God.

THE SICK ROOM

Sick Room Recipes

In some cases of acute illness, the digestive system must be allowed to rest as much as possible. For these patients, a fluid diet consisting of the following kinds of food and drink is often indicated.

1. Soups—both, cream soups and clear.

2. Barley water
   > 3 T. Barley, 4 C. water. Soak overnight, then boil for two hours.

3. Beef Tea
   > 2 lbs. cubed beef, 1 quart water. Let stand 1 hour then simmer for two hours.

4. Eggnog

> Beat 1 egg yolk well, add 1 t. sugar until light. Add egg white beaten stiff, stir well. Pour in glass, add a drop vanilla, and as much milk as glass will hold.

5. Oatmeal Gruel

> 1 C. oatmeal, 4 C. boiling water, 1 t. salt. Add oatmeal and salt to boiling water. Cook 10 minutes. Cook in double boiler three hours, strain, and dilute with milk.

6. Hot chocolate.

> 1 can Carnation milk, 1 can water, ½ t. cocoa. Heat, but do not boil.

7. Baked Custard

> 1 C. milk, 1 egg, 3 drops vanilla, ¼ grain sac charin, table salt. Dissolve saccharin first. Makes 2 small custards.

Raw juice is rich in enzymes (organic catalysts that increase the rate at which foods are broken down and absorbed by the body), thus enabling an immune system that is healing or recovering to absorb the valuable nutrients it needs more comprehensively.

Enzymes are destroyed when food is cooked or pro-

cessed, which is why fresh raw produce should consti-
tute 50 percent of meals that heal.

The destiny of nations depends on what they eat.

Tell me what you eat and I will tell you what you are.

HINTS AND TIPS

A little flour rubbed over the top of a cake stops the frosting from running off the cake.

Place a woolen blanket under the bottom sheet of your bed in the winter to keep the bed warm.

To prevent cakes from burning, sprinkle salt in the oven under the baking tins.

Heat lemons first before using; they will yield more juice.

Vinegar and water removes mildew and mold from shower curtains.

Borax and lemon juice cleans and deodorizes the toilet bowl.

Always put bacon into a cold fry pan, then turn the heat on.

Add lemon juice to water in which rice is to be boiled. The whiteness will increase and the grains will remain whole.

Hot honey poured over fried chicken. It's a different and delicious flavor.

To chop hard-boiled eggs quickly, use your potato masher.

Words to Live By

Take time to—think—It is the source of power.

Take time to—play—It is the secret of perpetual youth.

Take time to—be friendly—It is the road to happiness.

Take time to—love—It is a God-given privilege.

Take time to—read—It is a fountain of wisdom.

Take time to—pray—It is the greatest power on earth.

Take time to—laugh—It is the music of the soul.

Take time to—give—It is too short a day to be selfish.

Take time to—work—It is the price of success.

No Job Has a Future

The future is with the person who holds that job.

Success Has a Thousand Fathers

Failure Is an Orphan.

OLD FAMILY RECIPES

Homemade Bar Soap

1 C. clean fat
1 t. borax
5 t. lye
¼ C. soft water

Heat fat slowly until melted. Cool until 110°. Stir fat as it cools. Meanwhile, dissolve lye in water, cool to lukewarm (85°). Pour lye solution in fat very slowly in a thin stream with slow, even stirring. Now pour soap into prepared molds. Cover and keep warm for about 4 hours. Remove soap cut in bars and let stand for 2 weeks.

Hand Lotion

1 oz. of cologne
1 oz. glycerin
1 oz. alcohol
½ oz. traqacath gum

Dissolve gum in hot water, let cool, then add the other ingredients. Mix until all is dissolved.

Shampoo

Shave 3 C. of good soap into 4 C. of water. Cook until dissolved. Let stand till morning. Then add the whites of 2 eggs, stiffly beaten.

Furniture Polish

1 quart hot water
3 T. boiled oil
3 T. turpentine

Keep warm while using. Ring cloth out of solution and wipe over woodwork, then polish with soft cloth.

Tile and Tub Cleaner

Use baking soda to clean tub and tiles.

Dust Cloths

1 pint of hot water
2 T. of turpentine

Dip cloth into this, then hang to dry.

Burn Treatment Mix

The white of an egg mixed with equal parts of glycerin will relieve the pain.

Paint Remover

Mix ½ package of celluloid starch and 2 T. of lye in 1 gal. of water. Heat until it thickens, keeping hot all the time. Brush over paint or varnish, wash off with clean water, then let dry.

Joy Logs

Tightly roll and tie paper or magazines. Place 3 lbs. rock salt and 1 gal. water in a 5 gal. crock or glass vessel. Place logs in loosely as they will swell. Cover with solution and soak thoroughly, remove, and let dry.

Skin Moisturizer

Mix 1 t. honey and ½ banana. Mash and mix well. Apply to face for 15 minutes. Rinse off with warm water.

Facial #1

Beat the white of 1 egg. Rub in with a cloth. Leave on your face for five minutes, then rinse off with water.

Facial #2

1 egg yolk
1 T. honey
1 T. cooked oatmeal
1 t. fresh orange juice

Apply to face for about 15 minutes. Rinse off with cold water.

Mayonnaise Conditioner

Apply 1 T. of mayonnaise to your hand. Massage into hands, feet, and face. Rub mayonnaise into your hair, and wrap a damp towel over your head for 10 minutes. Rinse well and shampoo.

Windshield Washer Cleaner

1 qt. of rubbing alcohol
1 C. water
1 C. vinegar
3 t. liquid detergent

Sparkling Dishes

Add 1/8 C. of vinegar to your dishwasher. Vinegar cuts grease.

Pickle Juice

Don't throw pickle juice out. We use it for marinades, coleslaw, salad dressings, and barbecue sauces.

Fabric Softener Cloths

1 pt. warm water
2 t. fabric softener

Ring out small cloths in this mixture and place in your dryer. Can be used over again. Less expensive!

Drain Cleaner

Use ½ C. salt and ½ C. baking soda. Pour into drain, then pour 1 quart of boiling water in too.

Mustard Plaster

1 T lard
½ t. dry mustard

Mix well and make a paste. Apply to a cloth. Can be kept on all night without blistering. Good for chest colds.

Toothache

Rub a little oil of cloves on the gums, under the bad tooth on both sides.

STAIN REMOVAL CHART

Blood

Sponge or soak in cool water until color turns light brown. Then wash in warm, sudsy water. If it is an old stain, soak in 1 qt. lukewarm water and 1 T. ammonia.

Butter, Grease, and Oil

Scrape off excess. For washables, rub with liquid detergent and wash in warm, sudsy water. For non-washables, sponge with carbon tetrachloride or solvent.

Candle Wax

Scrape off excess with a dull knife. Place fabric between paper towels and press with warm iron. Remove color stain with rubbing alcohol or bleaching.

Chewing Gum

Rub with an ice cube and scrape off excess with a dull knife. Sponge with carbon tetrachloride or solvent.

Coffee and Tea

If milk or cream is present, first sponge with cleaning fluid. Then soak garment in cold water. If safe for fabric, stretch area over bowl and pour hot boiling water over the stain.

Fruit and Berries

Sponge immediately with cool water. Stretch over bowl and pour boiling hot water through it. Then dab with rubbing alcohol.

Grass

For non-washables, sponge with rubbing alcohol. For washables, rub in thick hot suds, rinse, and bleach if necessary.

Lipstick

First, soften with Vaseline. Then, if washable, launder in warm soapsuds. Sponge non-washables with cleaning fluid.

FASTING

Cleaning and Healing the Body

There is no other food better for you than raw vegetables, fruits, or juices.

Vegetables and juices are rich in enzymes, which help the body break down and absorb other foods. They also heal and build the immune system and absorb valuable nutrients. Remember that enzymes are destroyed when foods are cooked.

Raw juice cocktails that make up 50 percent of your daily diet will increase your energy and change your overall health very quickly.

Buy the best quality produce you can. Wash thoroughly. Remove all skin and seeds.

Fast with juices, *not* water. If you need to use water, only use distilled water.

Do not fast longer than five days. Diet the day before, with raw fruits and vegetables or homemade soups or broths. After your fast is over, no meats, grains, milk, or dairy products for two days.

Cleaning the body

Beet juice, cabbage juice, carrots, apple, parsley

Energy

Apple, carrots, parsley
I always add ½ an orange to this.

Fruit juicer

2 peaches, ½ lime, ½ orange, 1 banana, 1 T. Brewer's yeast, and ¼ C. distilled water

Potassium Juicer

Spinach, parsley, 4 carrots, and 3 celery stalks

Minors, or anyone with health problems or any serious health conditions, should contact their doctor before fasting.

TO ALL THE SPECIAL
PEOPLE IN MY LIFE

To Doreen, my wife; Dawn, my daughter; and Mark, my grandson. I would like to say thank you for all your understanding, patience, guidance, and support these past long years.

I could not have done it without you all.

To Bill and Starr Heckman of Capriole, Ontario: I thank you for some of your old wonderful recipes that are in this book

I would also like to thank Gerri Elliott of Kenora, Ontario, for allowing me to use some of her very old family recipes, too.

To all my customers, for your faith in the first book: a special thank you, too.

Arthur R. (Roy) Thornton

Arthur R. Thornton.
As a hunting and fishing guide in northern Ontario, Canada, for many years at a remote fly-in outpost camp, many of our customers would ask my wife or I, "Would you please give us your recipe for that shore lunch or dinner?" And most would say, "You should publish your recipes. They are great." So we did.

Have fun and please enjoy the book.
Arthur Thornton

listen|imagine|view|experience

AUDIO BOOK DOWNLOAD INCLUDED WITH THIS BOOK!

In your hands you hold a complete digital entertainment package. Besides purchasing the paper version of this book, this book includes a free download of the audio version of this book. Simply use the code listed below when visiting our website. Once downloaded to your computer, you can listen to the book through your computer's speakers, burn it to an audio CD or save the file to your portable music device (such as Apple's popular iPod) and listen on the go!

How to get your free audio book digital download:

1. Visit www.tatepublishing.com and click on the e|LIVE logo on the home page.
2. Enter the following coupon code:
   edef-d0f2-873e-fd5b-aa85-765a-ca71-65ce
3. Download the audio book from your e|LIVE digital locker and begin enjoying your new digital entertainment package today!